PLATFORM PAPERS

QUARTERLY ESSAYS ON THE PERFORMING ARTS

No. 27
April 2011

CURRENCY HOUSE

PLATFORM PAPERS
Quarterly essays from Currency House Inc.
Editor: Dr John Golder, j.golder@unsw.edu.au
Currency House Inc. is a non-profit association and resource centre advocating the role of the performing arts in public life by research, debate and publication.
Postal address: PO Box 2270, Strawberry Hills, NSW 2012, Australia
Email: info@currencyhouse.org.au Tel: (02) 9319 4953
Website: www.currencyhouse.org.au Fax: (02) 9319 3649

ISBN 978 0 9807982 4 1
ISSN 1449-583X
Typeset in 10.5 Arrus BT
Printed by Hyde Park Press, Richmond, SA
This edition of Platform Papers is supported by the Sidney Myer Fund, Neil Armfield, David Marr, Joanna Murray-Smith, Martin Portus, Alan Seymour and other individual donors and advisers. To them and to all our supporters Currency House extends sincere gratitude.

SIDNEY MYER FUND

Contents

AVAILABILITY *Platform Papers*, quarterly essays on the performing arts, is published every January, April, July and October and is available through bookshops or by subscription. For order form, see page 70.

LETTERS Currency House invites readers to submit letters of 400–1,000 words in response to the essays. Letters should be emailed to the Editor at info@currencyhouse.org.au or posted to Currency House at PO Box 2270, Strawberry Hills, NSW 2012, Australia. To be considered for the next issue, the letters must be received by 10 May.

CURRENCY HOUSE For membership details, see our website at: www.currencyhouse.org.au

Hello World!

Promoting the Arts on the Web

ROBERT REID

The author

Robert Reid is a freelance playwright and director based in Melbourne. The author of over forty works that have had national exposure, he is a founding member and artistic director of the independent theatre company, theatre in decay, and the experimental puppet company, terrible COMFORT.

Robert has regularly hosted the Meant to Be Spoken playwright readings for Tashmadada at 45 Downstairs and the Melbourne Writers Festival. His plays have been performed by Black Swan Theatre Company (BSX) and the Storeroom Theatre Workshop. He makes his mainstage debut at the Melbourne Theatre Company with his *The Joy of Text*, a 'satirical dissection of education and its discontents', which plays in June-July 2011.

He has been short-listed for numerous awards including the Griffin Award for *Portraits of Modern Evil* in 2007 and the Kit Denton Award for *The New Black* in 2009. *The New Black* was selected for further workshopping at the High Tide Theatre in Suffolk, UK in February 2011.

Robert's essay, 'Everyone's a Critic: Discourse and Power in Australian Theatre Blogging', which was short-listed for the 2010 Veronica Kelly Postgraduate Award, was the impetus for the present Platform Paper. He has extensive experience of the online world, having written theatre reviews (under the *nom de plume* of Danny Episode) for the blog Television is Furniture, and established the Australian Playwrights Group on Facebook. He has served on several Arts Victoria assessment panels, and only recently was appointed the new editor of *Australian Puppeteer* magazine, produced by UNIMA Australia. His most recent online project is Flashing 12 O'clock, a series of 'podcast' interviews with people in the Australian world of the arts.

Robert completed a graduate diploma in directing at the Victorian College of the Arts in 2000, an MA in Creative Industries at QUT in 2007, and is currently enrolled in the doctoral program at La Trobe University, where he is documenting the emergence of independent theatre in Melbourne since 2000.

Acknowledgements

I would like to extend my thanks to the La Trobe University Theatre and Drama Department for being so understanding about my tendency to over-commit to extramural projects. I thank in particular Julian Meyrick, Geoffrey Milne and Meredith Rogers for their continual and long-suffering support of both my academic and creative careers.

Special thanks must go to the wide range of experts whom I consulted for this paper. Although for reasons solely of length much of what they had to say, regretfully, had to be cut, all of them broadened and enriched my understanding of the field enormously and I am most grateful to them for allowing me to quote from our conversations: Görkem Acaroglu, Alison Croggon, Neal Harvey, Rand Hazou, Tom Healey, Ming-Zhu Hii, Olivia Illic, Natasha Jacobs, Tiffany Loft, Vanessa Paech, Mark Tregonning, Richard Watts, Marcus Westbury, and David Williams.

Too much credit cannot be given to the editor of this essay, John Golder, without whom I am certain to have written a heavily footnoted, excessively complicated manifesto on all things digital. I must also thank all the good people at Currency House for their work, not only on this essay, but for being an invaluable resource to the Australian performing arts community: to director Katharine Brisbane; to the members of the editorial board for surprising the life out of me by agreeing to publish me, and to John McCallum for generously replying to the odd, anxious, late-night email. In addition to these I must thank Chris Mead of PlayWriting Australia for his ongoing support and for putting me in touch with Currency House in the first place.

Lastly—and most importantly—I want to thank my partner, Sayra, for her support and for continuing to be patient while I monopolize the computer at home, build teetering piles of books about the place and occasionally burst into yet another lecture delivered to the uncaring universe!

Introduction

20 goto 10

> Dance, dance, dance, dance, dance to the radio.
>
> Joy Division[1]

In 2000, a Saachi and Saachi report to the Australia Council entitled 'Australians and the Arts' identified a general negativity towards the performing arts: in the eyes of the community at large they were arrogant, elitist and irrelevant pursuits. The reasons people offered for this negative attitude, the report found,

> relate to a lack of engagement, with many suggesting that they are not interested, or 'not into' the arts. This can be due to practical impediments as well as emotional factors, social customs and expectations, which present barriers to their engagement with and involvement in the arts.

'The most negative feelings', the research concluded, were 'associated with a sense of social exclusion.'[2]

That was a decade ago. Since then developments in online-communications technology, referred to generally as social media, have emerged that offer the performing arts powerful tools to address such feelings of disengagement and exclusion. Social media are Internet-based applications that facilitate inclusive social practices such as conversation, group creativity, collaboration and participation. Some of the best-known and widely used include Wikipedia, Twitter, blogs, Facebook, YouTube and Second Life. This essay considers their implications for the performing arts in Australia—in particular, the theatre—and proposes ways in which the performing arts can make better use of the archival, promotional and performative opportunities that social media offer.

The broader scope of the essay will encompass the relationship between the performing arts and their audiences. Social media are constituted and powerfully constructive of communities, and any exploration of the way/s in which they affect, and can be affected by, the performing arts must realistically also be an exploration of the recurring and ongoing relationships that the performing arts have with their communities.

According to American copyright lawyer and activist Lawrence Lessig, composer John Philip Sousa argued for the introduction of copyright law as a much-needed protection for artists against the interests of publishers and other less scrupulous sorts. For both Sousa and Lessig, the participation of the amateur in an art form promoted far more than individual involvement in that art form: 'Amateurism [...] was a virtue—not because it produced great music, but because it produced a musical culture: a love for, and an appreciation of, the music he re-created, a respect for the music he played.'[3] In so far as they present a significant opportunity to engage with and empower shared communities of interest and extend their networks beyond those already engaged, social media such as blogs, Twitter and YouTube can offer powerful ways of fostering wider cultural participation in the arts.

Social media can be thought of as a scale-free content-distribution network in which users generate and share their own content for free.[4] While it is certainly true that the content being distributed is often crude and amateurish, the emphasis of this content is not on professionalism, production values or 'quality'. Rather, these acts of online expression draw meaning from the act of participation and the dialogue of creation and response.

In essence, social media and the performing arts share a number of common practices: collaboration, creative expression and participation. Similarly, both satisfy a common need: the desire for community. They do this by facilitating communication, self-appraisal and shared imagining through participation. In this sense the performing arts themselves may be seen as forms of social media and, as such, be seen to have as yet untapped potential to lead innovation by making use of digital social media to foster stronger and more reciprocal engagement with the wider community.

1

No one knows you're a dog

> [G]enerations and generations of humans will live and die and experience nothing but gibberish.
>
> Cameron Woodhead[5]

During the course of last year, the Wheeler Centre in Melbourne held a series of open forums to debate the state of contemporary criticism in Australia. At the forum held on 8 September, the four panelists were playwright Stephen Sewell, director and historian Julian Meyrick, blogger and Melbourne critic Alison Croggon, and theatre critic for the *Age*, Cameron Woodhead.[6]

Two days later, on 10 September, in an article on the independent news website Crikey, Andrew Fuhrmann singled out Woodhead, describing the critic's performance during the debate as 'fopdoodle antics' and accusing him of acting 'almost as though he were deliberately trying to sidetrack the discussion'.[7] Four days later, on 14 September, Croggon published her thoughts on the incident at the ABC website The Drum.[8] Within hours New York theatre blogger George Hunka had joined the conversation on his blog Superfluities Redux.[9] Three days after this, on

17 September, the discussion was picked up in the United Kingdom by the *Guardian Online*'s theatre blog, Noises Off.[10] It had taken little more than a week for the discussion to attract international attention and to spark the latest contributions to the never-ending debate about the role and responsibilities of the critic.

A not dissimilar episode—featuring similar outbursts of online vituperation, but triggered by very different circumstances—prompts Clay Shirky to observe 'how dramatically connected we've become to one another [...] It demonstrates that the old limitations of media have been radically reduced, with much of the power accruing to the former audience.'[11]

Regardless of Woodhead's behaviour, or the substance and validity of his arguments, the response by a largely online community to the events of the Melbourne forum demonstrate the capacity of the Internet's widespread and disparate yet highly interconnected social networks to transform the local into the global. In short, as Woodhead himself put it in the title of his response, eventually published in the *Age* on 23 September, no matter where you are, 'If you're a critic on the Internet, everyone can hear you scream'.[12]

In the opening sentence of his *Understanding Media* Marshall McLuhan asserts that 'the medium is the message'. He goes on: 'This is merely to say that the personal and social consequences of any medium—that is, of any extension of ourselves—result from the new scale that is introduced into our affairs by each such extension.' For McLuhan, all media are extensions of our human senses, those senses that 'configure the awareness and experience of each one of us'. [13] In the same way, social media can be thought of as extensions of human awareness and experience, according those who have the means of access an ability to hold public, as well as previously private, conversations on a global scale.

For German philosopher and sociologist Jürgen Habermas, the public sphere provides the middle class (or the bourgeois, depending on the part of Europe under discussion) with a field of agency: a conceptual space distinct from the private, shared with authority and subject to rules of conduct, social mores, and the influence of public opinion, within which to conduct the ongoing negotiation of power.[14] Social media provide a field for similar negotiation between traditional and alternative modes of authority as is evidenced in the ongoing tension between 'official' or 'serious' arts criticism (as print-based commentary is usually characterized) and the contentious and 'unofficial' writing of bloggers and also general audience conducting public discussions of performance events via Twitter. Traditional distinctions between public and private discourse are regularly blurred by the use of the new technology, as indeed are issues of authority, quality and authenticity.

The source of Habermas's concepts of public and private discourse lie respectively in the Ancient Greek *polis* (city or citizenry) and *oikos* (household or family), states which were applicable only to the Greek citizenry: slaves, foreigners and other outsiders were excluded from the public sphere. Similarly, in the coffee houses and salons of eighteenth-century London and Paris, from which Habermas traces the emergence of the contemporary public sphere, agency was largely restricted to those with the means of access. In the same manner, economic, educational and cultural barriers to social media are real and should not be dismissed. While the open and participatory nature of social media provides a field for challenging traditional power structures, it should also be remembered, in light of the hyperbolic terms in which these discussions tend to be couched, that only 28.7 per cent of the world's population have access to the Internet.[15]

It was in 2004 that the Australian performing-arts world, at least a section of it, heard the word 'blog' (short for 'weblog') for the first time: that year Alison Croggon launched her blog, Theatre Notes, as a way of publishing comments and reviews, and of inviting discussion of performances she had seen. At roughly the same time, the use of social media began a significant worldwide expansion in popularity. The popular video-sharing site YouTube was launched in 2005, the social-networking sites MySpace and Facebook were made public in 2003 and 2006 respectively, and in its 2007 annual 'State of the Blogosphere' report, the blog-tracking website Technorati reported that it was tracking over 70 million blogs and estimated that 120,000 blogs were being created daily.[16]

Croggon's Theatre Notes was soon followed by a rapidly expanding rollcall of blogs including MinkTails, kept by Melbourne actor/theatre-maker Ming-Zhu Hii; Parachute of a Playwright, kept by expatriate playwright Ben Ellis; and The Morning After, kept by critic Chris Boyd. As more and more performance makers and audience members, anxious to share their experience of Australian performance, launch their own blogs, this community continues to grow.[17]

As communications technology has become more sophisticated and its cost to the customer fallen over the course of the last decade, these websites, and a myriad of their less well-known precursors and imitators, have presaged what Marcus Westbury, host of the ABC's *This is Not Art* series and chair of Renew Newcastle, describes as a cultural shift: 'I can't emphasize it enough. It's about recognizing that this culture now is participatory. It talks back, it feeds back, it has its own expectations and opinions. It's not going to be defined by a small number of experts telling it what to do.'

Such feedback is vital to the ongoing maintenance and sustainability of any system.[18] As social media continue to expand further into a global public sphere, they offer the performing arts an important feedback mechanism. However, to think of social media solely as an information-feedback loop is to underestimate their wider value. Social media offer the possibility for connections to be made within and between otherwise disconnected communities. Westbury recalls his introduction to the early precursors of social media, online Bulletin Board Systems:

> The classic joke is that 'on the Internet no one knows you're a dog'. Well, on the Internet no one knows you're fifteen. I remember being fifteen, being able to get into very grown-up discussions

> and dialogues with grown-up people, and being able to pass myself [off] as an intelligent, educated grown-up. Also it gave me access to an international community, at a very young age. I was talking to people from Europe and the States [while] living in suburban Newcastle. That was actually quite amazing. That's in a lot of my writing, I think, how culturally significant that is—to no longer be culturally, exclusively, anchored in place.

An emphasis on place is a recurring theme in discussions of social media. Social networking sites such as Facebook and Twitter and virtual environments such as Second Life are thought of as 'places' in which to interact with other users. These places have no physical reality, of course—if they have any kind of physical presence, it is in the billions of electrical charges that a computer interprets as content—but they do exist metaphorically in the shared imaginations of the users. For those who can gain access to it, this digital public sphere forms a shared conceptual space in which communities are generated by discussion. It exists neither here, nor there, but in the dialogue between. Social media, then, like any other shared metaphorical spaces—ritual, social or performative—are liminal.

2

The gaze of who we are

> Let him who has not photocopied thirty copies of whatever for an amateur production throw the first stone.
>
> Tom Healey

In 1981 Peter Holloway wrote: 'Each new generation of [Australian] dramatists has had to regain its craft, its Australianness, and its confidence from its own resources.'[19] Thirty years later, in the 2010 Philip Parsons Memorial Lecture, John McCallum made the point that 'the more new performance tools you discover the more important it is to go back to the past, to re-witness it and to re-configure it in all the theatre that you create. We forget our past at great cost.'[20] There's nothing new about the assertion that Australian theatre repeats itself out of ignorance of its cultural heritage, and the regular repetition of that assertion implies an entrenched culture of disposability. In last year's Rex Cramphorn Memorial Lecture, artistic director of Melbourne's Malthouse Theatre Marion Potts described the cultural reticence with regard to reflection and introspection that is the legacy of that disposability;

> We are still trying to capture this irrepressible culture in a shape and a size that was [*sic*] made

> for someone else, for a culture that may once have bottled all our colonial dreams, but that *is* in the end not us. We never developed a means of expression that allowed us to hold the gaze of who we are—let alone of who we are becoming.[21]

Common to each of these observations is an insistence on the vital importance of the shared cultural heritage of the Australian performing arts to their future development. One of the key practical problems facing anyone who wishes to build on this heritage is the issue of access.

Cultural memory is an imprecise term that can refer not only to inherited cultural practices, but also shared cultural capital. In my discussion here of the performing-arts community, I use it to refer to a broad scope of tangible evidence including performance texts, video documentation, individual company histories, documentation of artistic process, records of policy initiatives and philanthropic support, and the assorted ephemera associated with the performing arts. In many cases, the preservation of this shared cultural heritage has meant the sacrifice of its accessibility—kept in State library collections under restricted access, for instance. Much more of that heritage may already be lost.

Play scripts present an obvious and concrete example of the difficulties of preserving the creative works even of contemporary authors. Though Currency Press, Australia's oldest and largest exclusively performing-arts publisher, does an admirable job of regularly publishing a percentage of new Australian works, and some of the latest research into Australian performance, a far wider percentage of plays and research has historically remained unpublished and inaccessible. The problems associated historically with publishing drama for the—let's face it—pretty small readership in Australia are illustrated by the one-man publishing house, now sadly defunct, Yackandandah Playscripts. Founded in 1981 by Jeff Fiddes, and operating largely out of the lounge room of his Montmorency home in Melbourne, Yackandandah sought to provide access to plays that were unlikely to attract the major printing houses. Their inaugural publication was John Romeril's *Bastardy*, which

> no one was likely to do again and not many would read, but it was an excellent play that broke new ground and therefore was significant for both the present and the future. It should have been in print and easily available, not locked away in a government-run warehouse, its existence known only to scholarly researchers.[22]

Fiddes tended to deal directly with playwrights, 'calling and asking "what have you got for me?"' Likewise, the scripts were distributed directly through mail order or on-sold to local independent bookstores. The distributed networks used by Fiddes are for the most part the same ones through which social media operate today to facilitate the preservation of cultural memory, relying less on hierarchical business structures than on a network of social connections.

Based in Hobart's Salamanca Place (and occasionally a lounge room in Brunswick), the Australian Script Centre is an online resource that evolved from the much-regretted demise of the Salamanca Theatre

Company. First established in 1980 as the Salamanca Script Resource Centre, the Australian Script Centre offers a centralized portal to its own considerable library of digitized scripts, as well as the collections of other retailers of Australian plays, including Currency Press, Playlab, Full Dress publishing, Salt publishing and various others. The principal difficulties facing Tom Healey, the Script Centre's literary manager, are sourcing works and negotiating rights:

> Every single title has to be dealt with individually, and then sometimes via an agent. In some cases the writers are dead or a long way away, so it is very tricky. It's not as simple as grabbing it, scanning it and chucking it online.

Much of Healey's work, in the ten hours a week he is employed by the Script Centre, has so far focused on scouring the collection, identifying significant gaps and sourcing missing works:

> One of the biggest [problems] I found early on, and which I just managed ten months later to rectify, is that not one of the Keene/Taylor projects was there. I've since managed to get all forty of them as well as the rest of Daniel's writing. [...] I think, if any writer overseas is [asking], 'Okay, who's writing in Australia? Who should we be reading?', all of Dan Keene's stuff has to be there.

Simple availability, however, is not the only barrier to general accessibility. Also complicating the process is the negotiation of rights management for collaborative works and out-of-print early works or works published by companies that no longer exist. If Yackandandah Playscripts, for example, has given Healey headaches, it is 'because [their scripts] are out-of-print. [...] I'm still trying to sort out who owns what Yackandandah owned. Somebody does, but I don't know who it is.'

Lawrence Lessig writes of the scores of out-of-print works that, stored inaccessibly in libraries, are as good as lost: '[A]ccess is important because it teaches us about our past, and about the diversity of culture that lives around us. The first step of [*sic*] learning is listening.'[23] The growing library maintained by the Australian Script Centre offers a centralized repository of Australian theatre's cultural heritage and as such it also offers an important resource for contemporary artists, better enabling them to reinvestigate and reinterpret our shared past.

Beyond access to play texts, however, there is an even greater untraced wealth of historical information about the Australian performing arts in the ephemeral details of performance, direction, design, choreography *et cetera* that remains to be captured and documented. The AusStage project was established in 1999 by ADSA [the Australasian Theatre, Drama and Performing Arts Studies Association] with support from the Australia Council, PASIG [Performing Arts Special Interest Group] and Playbox theatre to capture and record more of this data.[24] Neal Harvey, Creative Producer for Melbourne Fringe and previously Research Fellow at AusStage, describes the project as an attempt

> to build a database that sits somewhere between Wikipedia and a library catalogue. The point of such a database isn't that it contains ALL the TRUE information. The point is that it is a starting point or launching pad for further information retrieval.

Harvey also describes how new developments might widen the scope of the project so as to make it not only of research use to the scholar and historian, but also of general interest to a general public:

> AusStage's evolution into the live data capture arena means that very soon it will begin to capture live, audience response to events. Those responses can be collected via SMS, Twitter or the mobile web [and] mapped, analysed and visualized in a variety of ways. Such data could be very interesting to audiences.

Indeed, coupled with automated online-user profiling and recommendation systems—such as those employed by online retailers like Amazon and user-generated tagging or book marking offered by websites like Digg and Delicious—live-audience tracking could also be developed into a powerful tool for better connecting audiences with a wider variety of performances.

While neither the Script Centre nor AusStage are social media in their most immediately recognizable sense, both rely on practices that are essential elements of social media and the production of online content: peer contribution, crowd sourcing and collaboration. Most importantly, they provide a conceptual space in which our shared cultural heritage can be expressed outside 'official' institutional contexts of authority and in which the wider community can challenge, interrogate and renegotiate canonical definitions of culture. Common to all such social media is the empowerment of the users to make meaningful contributions to the community and thereby experience feelings of ownership, identification and inclusion.

Access to our creative cultural heritage is vital not only for the connection it facilitates between historical works and contemporary practice, but also as a gateway between the arts and their audiences. Web-portals such as Theatre Alive in Victoria and Greenroom in Queensland go some way towards demonstrating the potential commercial applications for centralized online cultural hubs to connect and inform audiences about the performing arts. Site Administrator Tiffany Loft describes Theatre Alive as a response to the independent theatre community's need for 'assistance with marketing and promotion, [...t]he idea being that it's a free online promotional platform for companies to promote their work to a potentially larger audience than they can get already. [...] Essentially we have a what's on and who's who of independent theatre in Victoria.' Its hierarchically structured administration, however, necessarily limits the scope of Theatre Alive and it remains largely in a broadcast mode. Greenroom, on the other hand, a personal project edited and administrated by Queensland reviewer and blogger Kate Foy, is better positioned to take advantage of the wider possibilities for direct engagement with the community. Greenroom in turn, however, lacks the dedicated resources that allow a supported project like Theatre Alive to reach the broadest possible demographic.

The missing link between all these online information hubs is a collection of accessible written histories that would constitute a context for the entire broad spectrum of performing arts. It goes without saying that the economic obstacles to keeping such a project regularly updated and centrally administrated would be prohibitive, as was all too clearly demonstrated by the histories of Yackandandah Playscripts and the Salamanca Script Centre. The alternative to such traditional models is to harness a distributed network of volunteer labour using a wiki. From the Hawaiian word meaning 'quick', wikis are collaborative websites that allow users to contribute, review and edit content through a simple WYSIWYG (what you see is what you get) content-management system requiring next to no programming knowledge. A wiki, like much of social media, is closer to an oral than a written form, in this case an oral history.

A project that was capable of drawing together information already available at sites like AusStage and the Australian Script Centre, cross-referencing it with user-generated data captured by a performing-arts wiki and linking it to the functionality offered by Theatre Alive would be an invaluable tool for facilitating ease of access to the performing arts. It would provide immediate answers to the sort of questions anyone might ask prior to having a night out: What's on?, What kind of show is it?, Will I understand / enjoy it? An ability to access descriptions of a particular artist, their history and their work, linked to an ability to find reviews, images and video footage of previous performances and to perhaps read script samples of current work—these would be powerful contributions to building an audience's familiarity with the performing arts and fluency in their various languages. Such fluency is an important factor in lowering perceived cultural barriers to participation by the wider community and reducing the seeming otherness and irrelevance of the performing arts.

The energy and collective knowledge required to drive such a project is admittedly considerable, but its existence has already been well demonstrated in one of the Internet's most rapidly expanding conceptual spaces and the site of the Australian performing-arts community's most successful foray into social media, the Blogosphere.

3

Who are we to believe

> I am not a journalist. I don't go digging up sources, corroborating facts and claiming to be unbiased. I am not objective. I will tell you what I like and why, let you make your own decisions based on whether my tastes and yours seem to match.
>
> Steve Smart[25]

Though Alison Croggon might object to use of the word 'influential' to describe her work, she can hardly deny that over the last decade her blog Theatre Notes has become one of the most talked about, linked to and read blogs concerning Australian theatre. In a post entitled 'On Turning into a Crrritic', she characterizes her impetus to begin blogging as 'an irresistible loquacity, a desire to talk about the art stuff I see, which is married to the desire for interested interlocutors'.[26] It's this desire for conversation that separates the practice of blogging from traditional 'authorized' criticism. Though Croggon's blogs are highly articulate and deeply considered, they are usually only the beginnings of conversations, which develop both with her and, through her, between other contributors.

Blogging, the practice of keeping an online diary or weblog, has arguably been among the most successful and powerful aspects of social media to date. From its emergence in 1999 with the popular LiveJournal and Blogger sites, the practice has grown exponentially to the point where, as a form of amateur journalism, blogging has become a rival to mainstream print media.[27] The content of these blogs is as individual and idiosyncratic as their authors and, frankly, in the majority of cases is of limited general interest, written as they are for a very specific readership (the local crafting community, cat owners, *Star Wars* fanatics and so forth).

Blogs—particularly the most successful—exist within a complex network of communities drawn together by common interests. Blogs can be a powerful tool for creating agency within a specific community. At the same time, however, the practice of trading links and building community can tend to privilege those bloggers first to establish themselves. Assessing the development of online communities in digital space, author and former Director of Talks at the ICA, James Harkin writes:

> The blooming of millions of blogs is often considered a blow against the entrenched interests of elites, but things are not quite as simple as they look. The first bloggers to set up shop certainly found themselves in a level playing field, with each competing equally for the eyeballs of online readers. They were hugely dependent on attracting the attention of their peers in the blogosphere. Blogs don't usually advertise their wares, after all, and depend greatly for their traffic on attracting links from other weblogs that point readers in their direction.[28]

While Harkin is rightly sceptical of the notion that blogs provide genuinely democratic access to a worldwide platform—as he writes, 'New arrivals [soon discovered that] some were a good deal more equal than others and that the pecking order had been decided long ago'—it is a mistake to see blogging as primarily an alternative avenue to success in mainstream journalism. In the main, the aim of blogging is not to reach as wide an audience as possible, but rather to engage specific and usually fairly limited communities in discourses of shared interest. Just as Lessig reminds us that we 'learn by listening', so in the blogosphere we also learn by talking.

In 'Apologia', her first post for Theatre Notes, Croggon tells how one day it struck her that

> a blog that focused on theatre criticism would be a most interesting thing to do. The format is

> perfect. I can review whatever I like and, unlike reviews which appear in periodicals or newspapers, the commentary itself is always accessible for public record. Another interesting facet is a blog's interactivity, which gives reviewing the possibility of being much closer to what I believe it, ideally, is: an important part of the dialogue within theatre itself.[29]

In the open environment of the blogosphere it's easy to imagine the 'dialogue within theatre' that Croggon hopes for as one in which artists, critics and audience can all offer their opinions, share their experiences and discuss the reasons for the success and/or failure of particular productions. By means of open discussion, critic, artist and audience might all come together to contribute to the development of the country's theatre. In this ideal world the conversation would be conducted calmly, with respect and acknowledgement of difference. On the blogs, however, where the form encourages an immediate rather than a considered response, the opposite is more often the case. The insecurities and resentments engendered by the fluctuations of fashion in the arts are amplified into personal abuse and posturing on the blogs, dissuading artists from engaging in the discussion and thereby short-circuiting what could be a vital feedback mechanism between artists and the wider community.

Though Croggon welcomes bloggers who disagree with her: 'People who come and say, "Well, Alison, blah blahblah and I disagree", they're the people who make me lift my game, and I wish there were more of them.' On more than one occasion communities of blog readers have rapidly mobilized to attack, or even exclude, perceived difference and transgression. For example, in 2006 on her Mink Tails blog, actor Ming-Zhu Hii's negative assessment of the Short-and-Sweet Ten-Minute Play Festival drew an escalating response from supporters of the festival, culminating in threats of legal action against Hii and an eventual demand that she remove the offending blog post. In this instance Hii's right to her opinion was defended by other bloggers, including Croggon, who in their turn also drew abuse and threats.[30] No such defence was offered actor Neil Pigot, however, when he criticized Croggon's work on Theatre Notes in 2009. To her credit, when her readers leapt to her defence and turned on Pigot, Croggon directed them to her comments policy and reminded them that 'personal abuse is out'. However, this failed to stop her readers from making comments such as 'What have you done for Australian theatre, Neil?' and 'Perhaps you need to pull your head in', until Pigot retired from the fray, posting 'What have I done for Australian theatre? Clearly, not much.'[31]

Despite such instances of unpleasantness, Croggon regards the Theatre Notes community as 'pretty good on the whole':

> The conversation is pretty civil and that's because I make it civil. [...] You just have these really simple guidelines: don't call people names, and [...] no ad hominem [attacks], and it works.

The guidelines on which Croggon insists are a subtle means of controlling the conversation on her blog with a view to managing an apparently open, democratic discourse. Croggon exerts a fairly light hand in the exercise of her authority, rarely deleting a post wholesale and then presumably only when such posts cross a line of acceptability (being too abusive, libellous, nonsensical or irrelevant). Though no one familiar with her work would accuse Croggon of abusing her administrative privilege in order to censor opinion with which she disagreed, it is still she who decides exactly where the line of acceptability should be drawn, she and she alone who makes the decisions regarding the way in which the Theatre Notes debate will be shaped. How closely any administrator monitors the activity of her/his readers, when and how strictly s/he enforces her/his comments policy, these all shape the nature of the debate s/he hosts and the character of the community s/he attracts. Bloggers tread a fine line between preaching to the choir and complete anarchy, and bloggers as successful and influential as Croggon require sophisticated diplomatic skills if they are to maintain the balance. The question should be asked, then, whether the responsibility of monitoring a discussion forum that teeters regularly on the edge of a free-for-all is too much to be placed in the hands of a single individual.

Following the posting of critic Katherine Lyall-Watson's review of the Queensland Harvest Rain Theatre Company's production of *Cinderella* on her Performing Arts blog in 2010, the discussion was hijacked by a debate over the theatre company's Christian foundations. As the debate grew increasingly acrimonious, blogger TS suggested that, as the host of the blog, it was Lyall-Watson's 'duty '[…] to set the record straight! […] I think you should be speaking to the people who are being slagged off here and get the facts straight from them, before any more misinformation is allowed to be posted.' Lyall-Watson replied:

> This blog is a place for people to raise issues, debate points and get passionate. I don't want to police that and decide whose opinions are right and whose aren't. Whenever I have facts to hand, I will share them. […] You will see in previous posts that [theatre directors] Michael Gow and David Berthold have both commented to correct assumptions that have been made. If someone from Harvest Rain or QPAC would like to respond to any of the comments in this thread, I'm sure we would all be delighted to hear from them.[32]

The invitation to Harvest Rain or QPAC to join the conversation points to an important element largely missing from the performing-arts blogs, which would contribute significantly to their sense of balanced argument, the active participation of the artists under discussion. While bloggers' emotions can run high, as we have already seen, dissent is not necessarily a bad thing. 'In Melbourne there isn't a tradition of questioning reviews,' says Croggon. 'That whole thing about never answer[ing] reviewers because it's not dignified and doesn't get you anywhere is probably wise, but I can't see why that should be the case.' Making the occasional intervention in order to set the record straight, as artists like Gow and Berthold have done, is hardly the same as making a contribution to the debate. Only through a genuine and ongoing conversation between artist, critic and audience will blogging achieve its potential.

If the problem was caused by reluctance on the part of artists to engage with the blogging community, then there is evidence to suggest that things may be changing. In January of this year, reviewing the Melbourne Theatre Company production of David Williamson's latest play *Don Parties On,* on the independent news website Crikey, critic Jason Whittaker pulled no punches.[33] It was 'fat, lazy and stupid [...] a series of disjointed and desultory sketches, poorly plotted, embarrassingly overacted, neither witty nor wise'. Responses to this were divided: for some Whittaker's remarks were 'inhumane, nasty and personal', for others 'fantastic'. The subject of the online debate then shifted, from Whittaker to Williamson, to the play and its author's role in Australian theatre history. Later it shifted back again to Whittaker, whom a post from UPSHOT described as 'chattering and vacuous, agitated but without focus'. Other bloggers spoke up in Whittaker's defence, and the exchanges might well have continued in the same emotional and abusive vein until interest waned to the point where the site administrators called a halt.

But the debate was far from over, for it was at this point that the playwright himself, new to blogging but not to defending his work and reputation, pitched in, replying to both Whittaker and other posters. He noted, not unreasonably, that 'any disquiet' he might have felt up to that point had been 'about the sometimes vicious tone of the comment rather than its content'. Williamson's participation was welcomed by other bloggers: Theatre Lobby, for example, wrote, 'Good on you for responding. I think it's great that you're a part of the discussion and don't consider yourself extraneous from it.' The idea that his work 'should stand up for itself' and that he ever sought to 'refrain from comment [and lock himself away] in some sort of self-imposed ivory tower' was never one that appealed to Williamson, any more than it did, he asserted, to 'most artists. They're always arguing with critics and it's healthy.'

Although, with the playwright's appearance—and he came back time and again—the tone of the conversation assumed a greater measure of civility, there were the occasional exceptions. For example, one blogger, writing from behind the *nom de plume* of Talanoman—in the safety of the blogosphere we can become whoever we choose—was nothing if not blunt: 'Getting down and dirty in these columns isn't going to change the fact that some people seem to have decided that your best work is behind you.' The playwright let that one go through to the keeper.

This Crikey stoush, however, prompts some important issues out into the open, issues that involve social media. It is unquestionably 'healthy', as Williamson says, for 'artists [to be] always arguing with critics'. A topic for another day is his assertion that 'changing the critics' minds is rare'. However, when he asks, somewhat disingenuously perhaps, 'Who are we to believe [about *Don Parties On*]? Their collective truth or his [i.e. the general public's positive reaction or Jason Whittaker's negative one]?', he takes us to an issue of more fundamental importance, to which blogging is central: Who has authority in the critical debate, the 'authorized' reviewers in the traditional 'official' media, the 'unauthorized' contributors to the 'unofficial' online media of the new world or the response of the public measured at the box office?

Through their proliferation and the ease with which they can be accessed, in order to both read and contribute to debate, blogs have decentralized traditional, hierarchical structures of authority in the performing arts. Audiences need no longer sit silently in the stalls, their response limited to applauding or not, and dependent on the traditional media to decide how history should 'read' the event. They are free to speak their mind with impunity, as briefly or long-windedly as they will onto the screen. Nor need artists any longer feel that their voice may only be heard on the stage, that they have no right of reply to their critics. They are free to justify themselves as they see fit. If this means that in the future the role of the Internet critic might become more one of facilitation, mediating and moderating a direct conversation between artists and their audience, it also prompts us to ask what the nature and function of, say, the newspaper or radio critic might be in the future. As an ever-increasing number of Generation Y readers conduct more and more of their conversations 'privately' online, will the 'authorized' organs of criticism manage to retain their traditional authority?

While the aggressive behaviour sometimes demonstrated on blogs has been a factor in the exclusion of certain voices from the public discourse that blogging offers, other social forces are also quietly at work, shaping the conversation in which each particular blog community is engaged. Exploring the effect of group dynamics on deliberative knowledge creation, American legal scholar Cass Sunstein notes that 'groups often fall prey to a series of problems.

> They do not correct but instead amplify individual errors. They emphasize information held by all or most at the expense of information held by few or one. They fall victim to bandwagon or cascade effects. They end up in a more extreme position in line with the pre-deliberation tendencies of their members.[...] Indeed, deliberation often fails to aggregate information even as it increases agreement and confidence among members.[34]

Blogs, like wikis, are more closely related to an oral than a written practice, and a blog community might be thought of as a 'deliberating group' such as Sunstein describes. Without trying to come to definitive conclusions on issues, blog discourse does define its own set of cultural values, and in so doing is subject to the same subtly distortive effects that Sunstein observes. Croggon considers these effects, countering with:

> I think, in our own practices [...] we're all in our own silos. The Internet can reinforce that obviously, and people have talked about fragmented communities that don't talk to other communities, and that's definitely a concern, but on the other hand [...] I think often it works in this way that you find yourself coming out and talking to other people who are outside that community as well.

Though movement between such communities is possible for the active blogger, the communication between the communities themselves is in reality fairly limited. The communities of interest that gather, like-mindedly, around a specific blog tend to short-circuit conversation outside the defined boundaries of their shared interest, ultimately denying bloggers the genuinely open and challenging conversation they want. It can be difficult for new voices—particularly for new, dissenting voices—to make themselves heard over the background noise of a million other blogs, while older, more established blogging communities tend to dominate and control the conversation.

As far as the Australian performing-arts world is concerned, a valuable addition to the social-media landscape would be a dedicated review/blog aggregator, whose job would be to broaden the critical conversation beyond the established voices. For example, American arts journalist Douglas McLennan's blog aggregator and news site ArtsJournal facilitates access to a wide range of conflicting opinions, encompassing traditional media and bloggers alike, juxtaposing them in such a way as to create a genuinely multifaceted discourse. Paradoxically, amid the environment of phenomenal choice offered by the blogosphere, distinctions between concepts of mainstream and alternative and the traditional authority of the individual voice are reified at the same time as they rapidly shed meaning. The more contrasting voices are added to the conversation, the more fixed notions of value and quality are seen to be constantly shifting social constructs.

Ultimately the conduct of any conversation reveals as much about the speakers as it does the topic of their conversation. The individual social agency offered by blogging does empower bloggers to search out varying and contrasting opinions but, as collective entities, blogging communities repeatedly display a tendency to remain isolated—with the result that to a wider community of potential audiences, they risk appearing disconnected, fractious and combative. Blogging is a means by which the performing arts can be reconnected to a wider community that, according to the 2000 Saachi and Saachi report, had become disaffected and disengaged. However, if they are to be enabled to realize their full potential, then the conversations they host must become more broadly inclusive of differing opinion. As Croggon wrote in 2007, 'Maybe the biggest challenge we have as human beings is to negotiate our differences with respect rather than with big coshes.'[35]

To date blogging has probably been the most successful of the social media at gaining purchase in the Australian performing-arts community. Rapidly gaining ground in popularity, however, is the social-networking application Twitter. Unlike blogging, Twitter offers a severely limited format, Twitter posts (or tweets) being restricted to 140 characters or less, and individual tweeps (the collective noun for Twitter users) must 'follow' others in order to receive their tweets. Launched in 2006, Twitter was inspired by SMS, the mobile short-message service, as a way of communicating with a small group of users. According to founder Jack Dorsey, its name was chosen because, as ‘a short burst of inconsequential information’, it was like ‘chirps from birds’.[36] Such is its popularity in Australia that it is estimated that by last October more than 2.5 million Twitter accounts were held here and that we average more tweets per capita per month than the Irish, Canadians or Americans.[37]

Twitter has a number of unique characteristics: not only can its audience be hugely extensive—Lady Gaga, for instance, is supposed to have over 30 million followers on Twitter and Facebook combined—but it is able to address an extraordinarily flexible audience. At times tweeps appear to be posting for their own amusement, sometimes speaking into a void, sometimes in conversation with another tweep, and on other occasions addressing the entire Twitterverse (i.e. Twitter universe). What is clear about Twitter, however, is that personality and individuality are key elements. As writer, reviewer and host of Triple R’s SmartArts program Richard Watts puts it: ‘It’s the personal voice that’s much more interesting than the public voices.’

Referring to one of the *Age* film reviewers who writes on Twitter, Watts continues:

> He doesn’t follow anybody, he only uses it for self-promotion, or what reviews he’s written this week in his column on the *Age* website; there’s no sense of the social aspect of it. There’s no engagement, no argument, no discussion. [...] The companies that use it most successfully are the ones that adopt some kind of online persona, and they engage and

> they respond to people as opposed to having just a dry company voice.[38]

Twitter displays similar conversational characteristics to blogging and, in common with all social media, is again more usefully considered as an oral rather than a written form. Its immediacy and the individual nature of participation it offers lead to a developing familiarity that breaks down perceived barriers of authority. The roles traditionally reserved for cultural gatekeepers backed by massive capital and broadcast capability are, through Twitter and blogging, increasingly being recast in the mode of the individual and the personal because the position they hold is likewise increasingly less isolated. It is common on Twitter, in blogs and on the social networking site Facebook, to receive instant and immediate updates on both what members of the community are seeing and talking about and also what is happening in their lives. It's not uncommon to learn, for example, that Alison Croggon has a cold or that Richard Watts is going for a drink after a show: this kind of detail creates a sense of intimacy that subtly alters the perception of their position within the community. In short, their work becomes less an authoritative pronouncement and more a trusted personal recommendation. Summing up this aspect of social media, Watts says:

> Twitter is a very valuable marketing tool, a way of sending a targeted and specific message to a like-minded audience, but if you only use Twitter for that, you'll rapidly lose your audience. The value of Twitter is its way of engaging with an audience, and conversing and discussing.

Croggon agrees, adding, 'As soon as people feel they're being sold something, they [...] switch off. [...] It's still the case with most theatre companies, [who] think PR is about controlling an image, and that's just not possible anymore.' The inability to control can lead to huge embarrassment.

As an example, both Croggon and Watts cite the events surrounding an errant tweet sent out by an employee of London's National Theatre. In response to a particularly bad review by *Evening Standard* critic Steve Norris, the National's Twitter stream posted the following, 'Well, Steve Norris is clearly a giant cunt.'[39] Although within an hour the theatre had published an apology and attempted to restore their reputation by claiming that their Twitter account had been hacked, it was widely assumed that the more likely scenario involved a National Theatre employee mistaking the official feed for their own personal feed.

What is worth particular note regarding this event is the response from the twittersphere both to the original post and also to the subsequent retraction. Online digital and social media consultants The Nest analysed the event, noting responses to the National's first post by, for example, @DisAgg, who wrote: 'And to think I'd thought about unfollowing@ NationalTheatre for them being bland. Best. Tweet. Ever'; @LozKaye, who posted: 'For the first time ever I feel tempted to follow @NationalTheatre'; and blogger Megan Vaughan who wrote:

> For a moment there, you were my hero. The previously lack-lustre self-promotion that littered your feed was briefly enlivened, albeit with the word

> 'c–t'. You, our National Theatre [...] were human after all. Moreover, you were right! Steve Norris is clearly a massive c–t! Hooray for you! Hooray for the National Theatre! Hooray for passionate tweets about relevant issues![40]

In response to their clumsy retraction, the tide of support for the National quickly turned, as was demonstrated by @sarahmade, who posted, 'Oh, the poor employee at the @NationalTheatre who got their accounts mixed up. Hack? Yeah right. #cringe', and @andytfield who contributed, 'To be honest. The fact @NationalTheatre can't admit that someone said that shows everything that's wrong with that organization.' These responses demonstrate the new complexities in managing company PR, to which Croggon draws attention, and also the high value of the personal voice in the social-media landscape identified by Watts. Centralized and homogenous control of a corporate image is not only increasingly difficult, but in some respects counter-productive, as it reinforces a sense of exclusion. Conversely, the fact that 'a real human' is speaking through Twitter on behalf of the company reinforces a sense of familiarity, identification and trust. Blogging and Twitter are powerful media for promotion—self-promotion, particularly—but, as both Croggon and Watts suggest, unless it is to be ignored, promotion has to be located within a wider context of social interaction. Their power lies in the opportunity they provide to engage with communities and build inclusion and ownership. 'For Twitter to be used successfully', says Richard Watts, 'and for a company to have a successful online presence, it needs to move beyond marketing to a broader, deeper and more personable engagement with the audience.' To be effective, then, users of social media must demonstrate they are open to reciprocal relationships with cultural communities.

To regard blogs and Twitter simply as new kinds of marketing tool, and cast their most popular users as new kinds of cultural gatekeeper, is to relapse into old-fashioned notions of twentieth-century broadcasting. Traditional media work in one direction only: a single authoritative voice pointing the uneducated to culture and 'quality' entertainment. Social media work in both directions, not only providing audiences with entry points to culture, but also providing artists with entry points to previously elusive networks of audience feedback.

Those organizations that use social media to work with their audiences—that refuse to regard blogs as just another review, but actively join in the discussion of their work; that directly interrogate their audience via Twitter, and are prepared to listen respectfully to their responses; that use Facebook to share processes such as programming choices and artistic direction, that formerly were kept behind tightly closed doors—these will be the organizations with the best chance of reconnecting with those disengaged communities that Saachi and Saachi identified in 2000.An audience that feels it is not just a consumer but a valued part of the arts community is more likely to share those feelings of ownership with their own social networks. If only a few blogs reach a large but specific community of interest, then many more reach small but more diverse social networks. Likewise on Twitter—each tweep has its own followers, constituting widespread, closely interconnected networks through which information and (of particular interest to the performing arts) word-of-mouth recommendation can pass almost instantly. Considering the influence she has through the Theatre Notes community, Alison Croggon concludes:

> The whole thing, if it has power, it's through networks. I think people have a huge misconception about Theatre Notes, actually. It's influential, but only in so far as it's part of networks. It depends on who reads it, and then where that energy goes…

The conceptual spaces constituted through online contact as sites for shared remembering like Wikipedia, and shared discourse like the blogs, are fluid and communal. The communities that inhabit those spaces share participatory patterns, rituals and practices in a wide variety of ways that are social, collaborative and performative. Just as social media extend the opportunities for amateur participation in the arts to build fluency and familiarity, via wikis to learn through listening and via blogs and twitter to learn by talking, the possibilities social media offer for performance are exciting and largely unexplored possibilities to learn by doing.

4

For the world to see

> EagleCam had arrived on computer screens hot on the heels of the similarly themed PandaCam and just before the momentous launch of Cheddarvision, where an audience of nearly a million people logged on to watch a lump of English Cheddar mature.
>
> James Harkin[41]

Any place, conceptual or physical, where people gather is implicitly a space with the potential for performance, and the spaces created by social media are no different. The video-sharing site YouTube, for instance, estimates that 24 hours of video content are uploaded every minute and that over 2 billion of its videos are watched every day. Launched in 2005 and now a subsidiary of Google, YouTube claims to provide 'a forum for people to connect, inform, and inspire others across the globe'.[42]

'This is not mass media', says anthropologist Mike Wesch, discussing the culture of user-participation on YouTube. 'A large percentage of it is actually meant for fewer than 100 viewers.'[43] YouTube celebrity, he argues, is driven not by traditional star power, but by a community of users who share, reinterpret and redistribute the original performance. In the words of Doug Wolk, writing about the NumaNuma phenomenon and whom Wesch cites, participants on YouTube 'follow a ritual that's meaningful if not yet venerable: learning the dance, lip-synching the song, documenting their performance just so, making it available for the world to see'.[44]

YouTube is not constituted solely of user-generated content, of course: pirated commercial content sits alongside home videos as well as content developed and produced by major corporate media specifically for YouTube. In other words, YouTube is hardly an illustration of the democratization of the ownership of culture, as it might have us believe. As Media Studies professor Alexandra Juhasz has rightly written:

> YouTube could be a radical development in media because the video production of real people holds half of the medium's vernacular. However, by reifying the distinctions between the amateur and the professional, the personal and the social, in both form and content, YouTube currently maintains (not democratizes) operating distinctions about who seriously owns culture.[45]

But such scepticism is not for Lawrence Lessig, who responds by noting that the importance of social media is in the effect it has on the user as much as the culture. 'It enables a wider range of people to speak', he says. 'Whatever they say, that's a very good thing. Speaking teaches the speaker even if it just makes noise.'[46]

Social media, including YouTube, Second Life and a host of other peer-to-peer online media, offer to both professional and amateur alike access to a liminal space in which the relationship between passive viewer and active participant can be challenged, renegotiated and transgressed. Traditional boundaries on performance (temporal, geographical, linguistic etc.) collapse as the reach of social media expands through continuing developments in Internet technology, GPS and mobile devices. Performances have the potential to be accessed at any time from anywhere around the globe and can likewise invite contribution, participation and reinterpretation by a theoretically limitless audience. In this context the greatest changes social media may have to offer the performing arts are changes to the role of the audience itself.

As part of Melbourne's 2010 Next Wave Festival, Olivia Illic's multi-media performance company X:Machine presented a new work, *Straight to the 'Art*, a collaboration between Illic and digital artist Jarod Factor. It 'presented a cyborg version of myself on the Big Screen at Federation Square', Illic explains, 'and asked the GP [general public] to interact with the work by SMSing their thoughts, feelings or other.' The cyborg version of Illic, Circi Unit 1.0, 'responds' to the SMSs contributed by the audience by performing any one of a number of pre-recorded facial expressions or physical gestures.[47] Though audience members are offered an interactive experience by *Straight to the 'Art*, the work itself is reactive rather than responsive, programmed to search in the received SMS for key words or phrases, which in their turn trigger specific pre-recorded gestures. The absence of traditional devices such as narrative and character development allows for each such interaction, few lasting more than ten seconds, to constitute a stand-alone micro-performance, an automated individual transaction between human and machine comparable to a push-button educational display at a museum. It is a demonstration that, from a creatively engaged audience's perspective, there can be unconscious elements of performance even in the act of using a vending machine.

The call-and-response nature of *Straight to the 'Art* is a common solution to a mediated interactive relationship between audience and performance. The 2010 Next Wave Festival also hosted *The Short Message Service*—a collaboration between Jackson Castiglione (from the Perth-based pvi collective), Mish Grigor (Sydney-based performance group Post), Leah Shelton, (Brisbane-based dance company Polytoxic); and Lachlan Tetlow-Stuart—which placed two performers on stage ready to respond to, and presumably obey, any commands issued by the audience via SMS. It was billed as an examination of 'the ethical responsibilities of having control over someone else; how a crowd mentality can take over, and how fun it can be to have someone under your command'. Richard Watts, however, noted how 'fairly quickly' things

> got derailed into 'Tell us about how you lost your virginity' and [similar] fairly predictable kinds of [remark]. I didn't see the show, but [...] people sa[id that] the performers invited those comments from the outset, [saying:] 'Be frank, be rude, be brave with what you text to us and we'll respond to it.' So in some ways they invited that response, instead

> of encouraging more engaged and more challenging or creative texting.

Both *Straight to the 'Art* and *The Short Message Service* were notable for their replacement of traditional narrative with a partial or superficial empowerment of the audience. Both raise questions concerning the extent of an audience's genuine control over their participation in such situations and the extent to which the performance is actually manipulating them into believing that they are genuinely in control. Mik Frawley, posting on Crikey in response to Jana Perkovic's thoughts on Next Wave 2010, writes of *The Short Message Service*:

> [I]t possessed the raw potential of an audience 'controlling' actors in a space. Unfortunately the structure of the piece completely undermined the risk, as the SMSs were vetted and spoon-fed to the performers by the operators at rear of stage. [...] In *The Short Message Service* the mediation of the operators removed the ability for the audience to really have any more or less influence on the action than what made it past the keeper.[48]

Frawley identifies how, in the shifting relationship between audience and performance, the introduction of technology to facilitate audience involvement has the potential to place a significant amount of power under the audience's control. The addition of an intermediary between the *The Short Message Service* performers and the 'participating' audience was presumably intended to intercept intentionally disruptive contributions (what we might think of as cyber-heckling). This kind of mediation echoes the issue of control highlighted by Alison Croggon's and Katherine Lyall-Watson's blogs and may mask an increasing level of anxiety about the changing nature of the audience. Social media offer a space that is infinitely more flexible in terms of audience involvement, and one in which the performer/spectator relationship cannot be wholly defined in advance, instead becoming an ongoing negotiation between the two in the moment. Restrictive mechanisms of control tend to fail in such an environment, undermining the stated intent of the work. What may be called for then is a more open, inclusive and adaptive performance structure in which to situate the relationship with the audience.

For instance, X:Machine's production of *Serial Blogger* for the 2008 Next Wave festival fused YouTube, Facebook and live performance to present a series of narratives that gradually coalesced into one. When they work with narrative at all, performances that employ or are influenced by social media tend to work with multiple narratives, reflecting the range of interpretive and participatory options common to horizontal networks of online participation. *Serial Blogger*, said Illic,

> aimed at exploring the roles we 'play' online, the narcissism and the heightened sense of self we often project within cyber space. We set up four fictional characters whom we presented as 'real' to our online audience. Via a series of vlogs [video blogs] the characters got entangled in a web of passion, mystery and intrigue. The final vlog saw the Dark Prince, [a character] played by Mark Tregonning,

> setting up a room full of plastic, and inviting the other three characters into the performance space.

The experience of being an audience member at *Serial Blogger* was not a matter of simply purchasing a ticket, sitting in an allocated seat and becoming a passive witness along with lots of others: it was more like being part of an online social network. Invitations to 'friend' (in Facebook parlance meaning 'to join' a user's social network) the Dark Prince were distributed via Facebook to the networks of the performers and other creatives involved with the production. Once accepted, friends received regular updates on the characters' activities (status updates, emails, etc.) and were also directed to view vlog posts by the Dark Prince and the other characters in the performance. At this point spectators engaged in the event through their own computers (at home, at the office, etc.), watching short video postings from each of the characters in the form of YouTube vlogs. As such the event created a diffuse network of individual performance venues. *Serial Blogger* then made a transition from online experience to live performance, which took place simultaneously in several rooms constructed in the Bunker of the Arts House Meat Market. Illic again:

> The audience were free to roam the[se] space[s], and observe each of the characters in their own 'world'. The vocal text and sound score, [together with] physical gestures, were all delivered on top of [one an]other, creating a sort of aural symphony. [...] We also had four video stations where audiences could watch the vlogs of each of the characters next to their area. [...] Each of the rooms was projected in

> the various other rooms, so the audience could see the main action from wherever they were.

Even throughout the live performance of *Serial Blogger* the social practices that define social-media usage remained powerfully in evidence. Audiences were free to make their own path through the performance space, to make their own narrative connections and derive their own meaning from the performance. In essence, the audience were invited/lured into a space of narrative possibilities and then extended the freedom to negotiate that space and make of it what they might.

Conceptual spaces of shared narrative are not new; nor, it should be noted, is there anything particularly new about the practices of social media, apart from the technology itself. Projects such as Wikipedia closely resemble traditions of folksonomy and oral history; and blogging and Twitter rely on many of the same conversational elements as writing a letter or making a telephone call. Similarly, online performance has much in common with gaming and role playing, as Marcus Westbury has observed:

> [T]he possibilities for live events and live performance in real and/or virtual space seem limitless. [...] You look at something like a MMOG [Massively Multiplayer Online Game]—it's basically a giant bloody theatrical performance. There are thousands of people pretending to be a character, interacting with each other simultaneously, and that spills over into the real world. [...] I don't think it's too much of a leap to get those people and marry them up with the idea that you can create a live experience

> in the real world that's theatrical, [and] that allows them to participate.

One such MMOG, possibly the most widely publicized, is Second Life, which offers a graphically rendered three-dimensional virtual world that users 'experience' through a freely downloadable viewer.[49] Using the computer to input directional commands (from walking to flying), the user can explore the virtual landscape via their 'avatar', a digitally rendered self-designed representation of themselves. Users can also interact with the avatars of other users and, in so doing, generate genuine social connections comparable to those that constitute the Facebook, blogging and Twitter communities. Comparing these social interactions with those formed in more traditional MMOGs like World of Warcraft, authors Peter Ludlow and Mark Wallace observe:

> In open worlds like Second Life, There or The Sims Online, in which most of the 'game' has been stripped away, leaving something akin to a sophisticated graphical chat room, social interactions carry even more weight, since they are overwhelmingly the main ingredient of what goes on in such places.[50]

Görkem Acaroglu, Melbourne Workers Theatre's creative producer, is taking these liminal relationships a step further with *Exception*, a new work that she is currently developing. *Exception* explores the possibilities offered by Second Life as a performance space. Her interest, said Acaroglu, was in the way in which 'people in the First World or in the West' were using Second Life: 'I also was interested in the name Second Life and how it was being marketed as literally a 'second life', and that's how it was being used by people.'

In the main narrative of *Exception*, the politics of refugee and asylum seekers are examined, and comparisons drawn with the metaphors of freedom and new identity represented by Second Life. In its live performance, the piece explores the relationship between the actors 'operating' the avatars and the avatars themselves. In the original social-networking context of Second Life users create and operate avatars as digital extensions of themselves—and develop a relationship not dissimilar to that between actor and mask in traditional theatre, in which the wearer not only takes on the characteristics of the mask, but is also liberated by them. On the other hand, when the performance is contextualized by a total emersion within the Second Life space, it can take on disruptive and discursive elements that call to mind Augusto Boal's Invisible Theatre. Second Life is, within the terms of a subscriber-oriented online social network, a public space, and staging a theatrical event in that space further blurs what are already fairly blurred lines of demarcation between the real and performed. As with Invisible Theatre, in which the performed event is given the appearance of reality and spectators are not explicitly aware of the performative context, the constructed nature of events in Second Life can be used to destabilize notions of what is real, engender debate and even prompt spectators to action. For example, Acaroglu recalls that in its initial stages of development, *Exception* was entirely 'in world' (i.e. situated and performed wholly within the Second Life virtual environment):

> We created a detention centre in Second Life. We put Assim, the central character, in detention [...] and waited to see what happened. It was really interesting. We had communists, the Second Life communist party, coming in, [organizing] protests, making placards. Then we had the anarchists, from God knows where, breaking him out. First they brought him vodka [...] People couldn't believe it, saying, 'This isn't possible. It is not possible for someone to be in detention in Second Life.'

The work currently being done by artists like Illic, Acaroglu, PVI collective and Post, and by international contemporaries such as the UK-based Blast Theory, who have been developing interactive and digital performance works for over twenty years, extends performance far beyond what has hitherto been conceivable either in the real world or any virtual world. Furthermore, it holds out the promise of more extraordinary developments in the future. As far as the local, Australian, scene is concerned, this work builds on traditions of interrogating and renegotiating the border between audience and performance explored by companies such as Not Yet It's Difficult and Sydney Front. For all that, and despite obvious differences, cross-media work is no more permanent than any other more traditional kind of live performance, and it can sometimes struggle to make sustainable connections with communities of potential audiences outside of a festival environment. Similarly, as is frequently the case with still-developing art forms, it often finds itself misunderstood and has yet to establish for itself a secure place in traditional cultural-support structures, funding bodies and training institutions.

Innovation in social media is as often born out of open collaboration online between self-actuated and self-organized amateurs and professionals as out of the work of project-specific goal-oriented closed groups. The first step towards promoting and supporting innovation in performance that incorporates digital and social media might be as simple as the creation of a dedicated space in which to share and discuss new work, find collaborators for new projects and build relationships with new audiences. As part of its wider focus on the moving image, the Australian Centre for the Moving Image (ACMI) already clearly demonstrates the importance of digital art works. A project that focuses sharply on sharing new digital work and building new networks of creative participation would go a long way to extending the reach of social media as tools for performing artists. In short, what the digital performance community needs right now is not institutional, but infrastructural, support.

Defining the limits of social media as sites for performance is not easy. The more performance incorporates physical (as well as emotional and intellectual) participation, the closer it approaches role play. Participation is, after all, the defining characteristic of social media. The more use it makes of online technology for distribution, the more it approaches broadcasting. Exploration of the tensions between these two aspects poses complex and interesting questions about our relationship as audience to performance, our relationship as users to technology and our relationship as individuals to identity. We may even begin to see its ancestry in ancient practices, in communal events evoking the spiritual, or metaphysical, and in shared story-telling, ritual and trance performance.

The participatory element of social media offers more than the opportunity to become involved in the performance, it offers the opportunity to *become* the performance itself. Creating and sharing work, original, pastiche or collage, is an important element of this performance environment. The *Star Wars* kid, NumaNuma, Souljaboy and Free Hugs phenomena—all these demonstrate powerfully the popularity of online imitation, reinterpretation and re-inscription of amateur and home-video content. For Marcus Westbury, it's a matter of

> taking the skill set of the performers and applying it to the rules and conventions of the technology. [In] Elcho Island a couple of years ago [I] met with the Chooky Dancers, [...] a bunch of Indigenous guys who shot a dance performance in a basketball court in a remote island off Arnhem Land. A million YouTube hits later they've toured all around the world.

YouTube and its emulators offer users a space in which to create short works and share them among their individual social networks and the wider world. Active communities of shared performance exist in Second Life, and communities of shared narrative exist through fanfic websites (in which fans of popular films or TV series create stories and art works inspired by and/or set in specific pre-defined narrative environments). John Philip Sousa would acknowledge these as 'communities of amateur creativity', which build creative competency and fluency, key elements to the development of an ongoing engagement with the creative and performing arts and the highlighting of their relevance. In this endeavour the quality of the work performed matters less than its ability to engage and empower its audience. It's that participation, being invited to play an active role in the creative act, to 'come and play', that matters most. Shared conceptual spaces, be they real or virtual, require the active participation of two (or more) participants. An imaginative investment must be made by both performer and audience for the transaction of creative expression to have any meaning. Such an investment is more engaging when both parties feel they are essential to the transaction.

Conclusion

The safety of like minds

10 Print 'Hello World!
20 goto 10[51]

Somewhat unexpectedly, some of the observations made in the foregoing pages regarding the practices of social media and the possibilities they offer for self-definition and expression are echoed in a recent article by Hilary McPhee:

> Self-definition is still the great-unfinished cultural project and always will be—but without contributions from our changing population we are talking only to those who share the same perspective and who are invited into our privileged and privatized cultural spaces. Collective purpose has to be rediscovered and celebrated as an opportunity rather than a threat. The safety of like minds is a delusion.[52]

The opening of privileged cultural spaces to difference and dissent, which McPhee sees as vital to the project of self-definition, is just as important in the cultural as in the political sphere, and social media offer a powerful mechanism by which to do so. The process of self-definition is not so much one that reaches a conclusion, as one that is ongoing and carried out in conversation: the more inclusive the conversation, the more complex, surprising and useful in the moment the changing definition will be.

This essay has looked in turn at the archival, discursive and performative uses to which contemporary social media are put: projects like the Australian Script Centre and AusStage archive our shared histories; the blogosphere and Twitterverse provide a space in which contemporary practice can be discussed; and projects like *Exception* and X:Machine demonstrate the potential for digitally reinterpreting and sharing the act of performance. In short, social media offer us new and valuable tools with which to re-discover who we were, who we are and who we can be.

In closing, it is worth noting the caveat issued by authors and business-strategy consultants Don Tapscott and Anthony Williams:

> Companies can reach beyond their walls to sow the seeds of innovation and harvest a bountiful crop. Indeed, firms that cultivate nimble, trust-based relationships with external collaborators are positioned to form vibrant business ecosystems that create value more effectively than hierarchically organized systems. [...] Those who fail to grasp this will find themselves ever more isolated—cut off from the networks that are sharing, adapting, and updating knowledge to create value.[53]

It is these networks, identified by Tapscott and Williams as 'creating value by sharing', which offer the performing arts the greatest long-term potential for growth. As recently as January this year the magazine *Wired* began forecasting the evolution of social media into social commerce, identifying sites like Groupon, Lockerz and Blippy as its precursors.[54] Social-commerce practice leverages the interconnectedness of social networks to create what Groupon calls 'collective buying power',[55] in which discounted products or services are offered in exchange for individual promotion of that product throughout a user's social network. The marketing implications for the performing arts are obvious but, being essentially sponsored social practices, they will rely on a sense of genuine goodwill towards the product or service to be successful.

It is by genuine, open interaction in the forums offered by social media that this goodwill can be fostered. As a hypothetical example, imagine a State-theatre company that engages its audience regularly in public conversations about their work on their blogs and Twitter streams, and that offers discounted tickets to anyone willing to have their purchase broadcast through their Twitter and Facebook networks. Every Facebook friend and Twitter follower would know that someone in their immediate social group was talking to the people behind this company's walls and was about to attend one of their shows. The more commonplace such discussions and alerts become, the less alien the performing arts seem.

Beyond simply increasing the number of bums on seats, the conversation between artists and audience that social media make possible has the power to affect the performing arts themselves. What unexpected directions might the performing arts explore, if they engage seriously with their audiences via social media and involve them in decisions previously reserved for a privileged and solitary, albeit gifted and experienced, few? What might happen if conductors began using Facebook to discuss and debate with their audience which piece their orchestra should play; if choreographers began using YouTube to create works that anyone could perform, at home or together with the dancers as they performed that night; if artistic directors began using Twitter to invite input regarding the season's repertory? While no one would argue for the complete surrender of creative control to public plebiscite, the use of social media (blogs, Twitter, Facebook, YouTube, etc.) to include the wider community in the creative process is an important step towards breaking down the perceived elitism and irrelevance of the performing arts. As the 2000 Saachi and Saachi report, with which this essay began, concluded: 'Personal involvement is a key to helping people overcome a lack of engagement and a sense of exclusion.'[56]

Do I believe that social media offer a miraculous remedy for the ills that currently beset the performing arts in contemporary Australia? No, of course not. The addition to the online environment of one more blog aggregator, one more wiki or one more YouTube channel is hardly likely to result in an instantaneous dramatic surge of eager spectators through the doors of the mainstream or independent performing-arts companies. It will take more than new technology to empower audiences to see themselves as participants in, and not just consumers of, the performing arts. It will take time and a process of re-establishing familiarity and rebuilding trust.

'Nothing on the Internet stays the same', said Alison Croggon during our interview, and it's a sentiment worth repeating here. Such is the nature of the Internet that new developments can occur with phenomenal speed, so rapidly in fact that it's unwise to regard as definitive anything written on or about the Internet. What I write today could well be rendered obsolete by the innovations of tomorrow.

To each of my interviewees I put the same question: What is the nature of your relationship with your computer?—anticipating that they might estimate the time they spent using social media or connected to their digital community (via the Internet or portable/mobile device). Blogger/performer and social-media entrepreneur Ming Zhu-Hii's reply was: 'I carry my iPhone with me everywhere, and I take my laptop home at night. I try not to turn it on, on Sundays. It's hard.' Natasha Jacobs, who is a performer and administrator of the Facebook page We Love Melbourne Theatre, declared herself to be 'completely addicted to being accessible. My iPhone is always with me. If I lost either [my computer or mobile], I'd cry.' Richard Watts confessed that 'it's gotten to the point where the first thing I do in the morning, pretty much, is check my email, see if there's anything urgent, jump on Facebook to see if there are any important messages and then check Twitter. Usually I do that even before I get in the shower.'

Since each of my respondents was chosen for their close involvement with social media, perhaps they shouldn't be regarded as 'your average users'. However, their answers certainly reflect a general need that is currently being fulfilled, at least partially, by social media. The desire for engagement, conversation and participation is a desire for contact with community. James Harkin writes of these patterns widely observed among users of social media world-wide:

> Whatever guilt-ridden users of the Internet might think, it makes little sense to think of them as addicted in the way that people become chemically dependent on heroin or nicotine. A better comparison is with the time that people spend watching television. Many of us still watch a lot of TV, but few would argue that it is addictive in any meaningful sense. What it does for the most part, however, is to supply its audience with visual stories of different kinds. [...] The time we spend

> chattering with other humans on the web or via our mobile phones, however, is something else entirely. In this new medium we may still be searching out stories [...], but what we get are other people.[57]

Space limitations prevent any exploration of other important issues for social media and the performing arts, such as digital-rights management and the creative commons, online privacy, equity and the digital divide. Not that these issues have escaped critical attention: Googling the above topics as keywords will generate plenty of discussion. On the other hand, topics such as the digital media and the performing arts in Australia and the social practices they facilitate have not been fully addressed. The present essay is a modest contribution to what yet remains to be written.

In 2006, Harvard law professor Yochai Benkler wrote:

> In the past decade and a half, we have begun to see a radical change in the organization of information production. Enabled by technological change, we are beginning to see a series of economic, social, and cultural adaptations that make possible a radical transformation of how we make the information environment we occupy as autonomous individuals, citizens, and members of cultural and social groups.[58]

The information environment shared by the performing arts community in Australia is still open to adaptation and re-inscription. The burgeoning field of app development, for example, in which individual internet-based applications are developed for use outside the common web-browser (most familiar from iPhone and other touch-screen based technology), may yet provide companies and artists with the incentive to innovate and the ability to control and monetize individual access to new media. For example, the Melbourne and Sydney international arts festivals and Melbourne Fringe have already begun deploying their own apps as interactive program guides and ticketing resources. The same field, however, may represent a gradual corporate enclosure of what to date has been a relatively open access platform. Those communities that can successfully negotiate between the benefits and drawbacks of open access and closed profit incentives will in all likelihood drive the development of new models of sustainability and innovation in the performing arts and the wider field of communication.

Of the potential futures for the performing arts and their promotion by and integration with online social practice, Ming-Zhu Hii says:

> Social media are ever-changing. If we are really going to implement something lasting, significant, and useable by a broad range of people, we're going to have to help EVERYONE get over the cringe which accompanies fear of a quickly changing landscape. [...] We need to use it as a tool to build artists and audiences up, not cut them down.

To achieve this kind of potential inclusivity, which social media make possible, it will be necessary to challenge centrist notions of amateur and professional, artist and audience, performance and participation. In the words made famous by Mike Wesch's YouTube video, *The Machine is Us/ing Us*;

> We'll need to rethink a few things... [59]

Endnotes

1 'Transmission', Transmission EP, Factory Records, 1979.
2 P. Costantoura, *Australians and the Arts* (Australia Council: Surry Hills, 2000), p. 20.
3 *Remix* (Harmondsworth: Penguin, 2008), p. 25.
4 J. Hartley, *//the_uses_digital_literacy* (St Lucia, Qld: QUP 2009).
5 'If you're a critic on the internet, everyone can hear you scream', at http://cameronwoodhead.com/archives/2010/09/ (accessed 29 January 2011).
6 A video of this event can be found online at http://wheelercentre.com/videos/video/critical-failure-theatre/ (accessed 29 January 2011).
7 A. Furhmann at http://blogs.crikey.com.au/curtain-call/2010/09/10/histrionica-critical-failure-on-theatre/ (accessed on 20 January 2011).
8 Alison Croggon, 'The return of the amateur critic', at http://www.abc.net.au/unleashed/20038.html (accessed 20 January 2011).
9 'Alison Croggon on criticism and the Internet', at http://www.superfluitiesredux.com/2010/09/14/alison-croggon-on-criticism-and-the-internet' (accessed 19 January 2011).
10 C. Wilkinson, 'Netizens of the world unite', at http://webcache.googleusercontent.com/search?q=cache:kHbt4tGgYJcJ:www.guardian.co.uk/stage/theatreblog/2010/sep/17/netizens-unite-theatre-

blogs+critical+failure+guardian&cd=1&hl=en&ct=clnk&gl=au (accessed 19 January 2011).

11 *Here Comes Everybody: the Power for Organising without Organisations* (New York: Penguin, 2008), pp. 11-2.

12 'If you're a critic on the Internet' (accessed 29 January 2011).

13 *Understanding Media: the Extensions of Man* (New York: McGraw Hill, 1964: reissued Cambridge, Mass.: MIT Press, 1994), p. 7.

14 *The Structural Transformation of the Public Sphere* (London: Polity, 1989).

15 See http://www.Internetworldstats.com/stats.htm (accessed 16 December 2010).

16 See Wikipedia entries for YouTube, MySpace and Facebook, at respectively, http://en.wikipedia.orgwiki/You_tube; http://en.wikipedia.org/wiki/Myspace and http://en.wikipedia.org/wiki/Facebook_and_technorati; D. Sifry, 'State of the live web' (April 2007), at http://www.sifry.com/alerts/archives/000493.html (accessed 16 December 2010).

17 See N. Harvey, H. Grehan and J. Tompkins, '"Be thous familiar, but by no means vulgar": Australian Theatre Blogging Practice', *Contemporary Theatre Review*, 20.1 (2010), pp. 109-19.

18 See N. Wiener, *Cybernetics: Control and Communication in the Animal and Machine* (Cambridge, Mass.: MIT Press, 1961).

19 *Contemporary Australian Drama* (Sydney: Currency Press, 1981), p. xvi.

20 'Putting it back together and getting it on the road: Australian theatre in the 21st century', at http://www.belvoir.com.au/CustomContentRetrieve.aspx?ID=1084123 (accessed 28 November 2010).

21 Available at http://www.malthousetheatre.com.aumanaged_code/uploads/Transcript%20-%202010%Rex%20

cramphorn%20Memorial&20Lecture&20Marion%20Potts%20.pdf (accessed 28 November 2010).

22 M. Leehy, 'Yakarandah Playscripts: a Publishing House in Progress', *Publishing Studies*, no. 2 (Autumn 1996), pp. 38-43.

23 *Remix*, p. 106.

24 See the Ausstage website at http://www.ausstage.edu.au/ausstage.jsp?xcid=93 (accessed 30 November 2010).

25 Review of *Oh Well Never Mind Bye* by Red Stitch Actors Theatre, 6 October 2010, at http://www.rhum.org.au/index.php?option=com_content&view=article&id=1339:theatre-review-oh-well-never-mind-bye-red-stitch-actors-theatresteven-lally-gary-abrahams-wwwredstitchnet-venue-rear-2-chapel-street-st-kilda-3183-dates-oct-6-nov-6-2020&catid=35:article&Itemid=109 (accessed 29 January 2011).

26 http://webcache.googleusercontent.com/search?q=cache:RK7QZQpwMDcJ:theatrenotes.blogspot.com/2009/08/om-turning-into-crrritic.html+theatrenotes+%22stuff+i+see&22&cd=1&hl=en&ct=clnk&gl=au (accessed 16 December 2010).

27 See http://en.wikipedia.org/wiki/History_of_blogging and http://technorati.com/ (both accessed 29 January 2011).

28 *Cyburbia* (London: Little, Brown, 2009), pp. 120-1.

29 http://theatrenotes.blogspot.com/2004/06/apologia.html (accessed 29 January 2011).

30 For Mink Tails versus Short'n'Sweet, see http://chris-boyd.blogspot.com/2006/12/sour-grapes-of-wrath-shortsweet.html (accessed 29 January 2011).

31 For Theatre Notes versus Neil Pigot, see http://theatrenotes.blogspot.com/2009/09/response-from-neil-pigot.html (accessed 29 January 2011).

32 K. Lyall-Watson, 'Cinderella meets Prince', Our Brisbane, at http://webcache.googleusercontent.com/

search?q=cache:63UgglT9vMAJ:www.ourbrisbane.com/blogs/performing-arts/2010-01-08-cinderella-meets-prince%3Fpage%3D1+%22If+someone+from+Harvest+Rain+or+QPAC+would+like+to+respond+to+any+of+the+comments+in+this+thread+,+%22cd=1&hl=en&ct=clnk&gl=au&source=www.google.com.au (accessed 29 January 2011).

33 'Who's aspirational now? Williamson's Party as vapid as the times', Crikey (14 January 2011), at http://www.crikey.com.au/2011/01/14/whos-aspirational-now-williamsons-party-as-vapid-as-the-times/ (accessed 29 January 2011).

34 *Infotopia* (New York: OUP, 2006), p. 14.

35 'A confession of sorts', Theatre Notes (13 August 2007), at http://theatrenotes.blogspot.com/2007/08/conferssion-of-sorts.html (accessed 7 March 2010).z

36 See http://en.wikipedia.org/wiki/Twitter (accessed 20 January 2011).

37 Amanda Hooton, 'A little birdie told me...', *Sydney Morning Herald*, 22 January 2011, *Good Weekend*, p. 11.

38 R. and S. Buchanan, 'National Theatre's Twitter screw-up: what we can learn from other people's mistakes', The Nest (6 October 2010), at http://www.wearethenest.com.au/index.php/tag/training/ (accessed 29 January 2011).

39 http://topsy.com/twitter.com/nationaltheatre/status/2214514314 (accessed 9 February 2011).

40 'An open letter to the marketing dude at the National Theatre who posted 'cunt' to their Twitter account', Synonyms for Churlish, at http://synonymsforchurlish.tumblr.com/post/1013544623 (accessed 29 January 2011).

41 *Cyburbia*, p. 110.

42 See http://www.youtube.com/t/press_statistics (accessed 29 January 2011).

43 See http://www.youtube.com/watch?v=TPAO-IZ4_hU (accessed 29 January 2011).

44 'The syncher, not the song', at http://wwww.believer-mag.com/issues/200606/?read=article_wolk (accessed 16 December 2010).

45 'Learning the five lessons of YouTube: after trying to teach there, I don't believe the hype', *Cinema Journal*, 48.2 (Winter 2009), pp. 149-50.

46 *Remix*, p. 132.

47 A video compilation of the responses may be seen at http://www.youtube.com/watch?v=k_QKJgUllRC&feature=related (accessed 29 January 2011).

48 'Riding the Next Wave to the half-baked theatre', Crikey (1 June 2010), at http://blogs.crikey.com.au/curtaincall/2010/06/01/riding-the-next-wave-to-half-baked-theatre/ (accessed 29 January 2011).

49 See http://secondlife.com/ (accessed 29 January 2011).

50 *The Second Life Herald: the Virtual Tabloid that Witnessed the Dawn of the Metaverse* (Cambridge, Mass.: MIT Press, 2007), p. 21.

51 'Hello World' and the 'goto' command are common elements of BASIC programming language, used traditionally in introductory tutorials in computer programming. See http://en.wikipedia.org/wiki/Hello_world/ (accessed 29 January 2011).

52 'Timid minds', *Meanjin Quarterly*, available online at http://meanjin.com.au/editions/volume-69-number-4-2010/article/timid-minds/ (accessed 29 January 2011).

53 *Wikinomics: How Mass Collaboration Changes Everything* (New York: Portfolio, 2008), p. 15.

54 D. Rowan and T. Cheshire, 'Commerce gets social', *Wired UK* (February 2011).

55 See http://www.groupon.com/learn and

http://www.youtube.com/watch?v=3FN-ENgWO81&feature=player_embedded (accessed 30 January 2011).

56 Costantoura, p. 20.

57 *Cyburbia*, p. 17.

58 *The Wealth of Networks* (Harvard: Yale UP, 2006), p. 1.

59 At http://www.youtube.com/watch?v=mxOSk0VYy28 (accessed 30 January 2011).